WHY DO
plants grow in spring?

By Helen Orme

helping to explain
plant life cycles

WHY DO
plants grow in spring?

tick tock
MEDIA

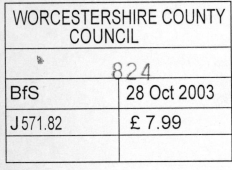
Copyright © ticktock Entertainment Ltd 2003

First published in Great Britain in 2003 by ticktock Media Ltd.,

Unit 2, Orchard Business Centre, North Farm Road, Tunbridge Wells, Kent, TN2 3XF

We would like to thank: Lorna Cowan, Bob Press at The Natural History Museum and Elizabeth Wiggans.

ISBN 1 86007 384 0 pbk

ISBN 1 86007 390 5 hbk

Printed in Egypt

A CIP catalogue record for this book is available from the British Library.

CONTENTS

Any words appearing in the text in bold,
like this, are explained in the Glossary.

Have you noticed that in the summer there are more plants and flowers in your garden?

Winter   Spring   Summer

In **winter** not much happens in the plant world.

But when the **spring** comes there are more hours of sunlight each day. The air and soil warm up. Plants know that this is the best time of year to get busy.

But where have the plants been hiding all winter?
Why do they need **insects** to help them in **summer**?
And why do plants have flowers?

5

What happens to plants in spring?

In **spring**, plants like daffodils, bluebells and hyacinths grow from **bulbs**.

Daffodil bulbs

Hyacinth flowers

Bulbs stay underground all year. In spring they push new **shoots** through the soil.

What do you think bulbs are made of? (answer on page 23)

The shoots grow into plants.

Daffodil shoot

Daffodil flower

Bulb plants grow flowers, but their most important job is making food for the bulb, using **energy** from sunlight.

6

Trees are the biggest plants of all. In the spring they grow new leaves.

Bluebells

Woodland plants, like bluebells, flower early in the spring before the trees get their leaves and shade the ground.

In spring you can see new plant shoots everywhere!

What happens to plants in summer?

a) They go on holiday

b) They shrivel up and die

c) They grow bigger and produce flowers

(You will find the answer on the next page.)

What happens to plants in summer?

Summer is the best time for most plants to grow and produce flowers.

In summer the days are longer so there is more sunlight.

Plants need sunlight. It helps them to make their own special food.

Do you think trees have flowers?
(answer on page 23)

By summer, all the new plant **shoots** have grown into plants.

Lots of the plants grow flowers during the summer.

All the flowers on the **spring bulb** plants have died. But the leaves carry on growing to make more food for the plant. The food is **stored** in the bulb ready for next spring.

Lots of **insects** like the warm summer weather too.

Butterfly eggs

Butterfly

They lay their eggs on plants in the summer, and get **pollen** from the plant's flowers for food.

Some flowers are tiny. Some are big and easy to see. Why are flowers important?

a) They make the garden look pretty

b) They produce seeds

c) Animals like to eat them

Why are flowers important?

Flowers produce **seeds** that help the plant to make new plants!

Flowers contain a special dust called **pollen.**

Pollen

Plants need pollen from another plant like themselves to help make seeds. The seeds will grow into new plants.

But plants need help to spread their pollen.

One way to get help is to use **insects**. The plant's flowers **attract** the insects.

Some flowers have a smell that insects like. Others have bright colours. The insects come to the plant to get **nectar.**

Which insects do you think are good at collecting and carrying pollen?

(answer on page 23)

When they land on the flower they get covered in pollen.

Without knowing, the insect carries the pollen from one plant to another. Now the plant can make its seeds.

What do seeds look like?

a) They are round and purple

b) All seeds are different

c) They are small and red

What do seeds look like?

There are many different kinds of **seeds**. When a plant is **in bloom** you can't see the seeds.

Sunflower in bloom

Seeds

Ripe sunflower seeds

But after the flower has faded, the seeds grow bigger. They become **ripe**.

Some seeds grow inside **pods**.

Seed pod

Some are hidden inside a fleshy fruit.

Others grow inside their own spiny cases.

Sometimes we make food from seeds. We **grind** up wheat seeds to make flour. Bread, cakes and biscuits are made from flour.

But seeds are not just there for people to eat.

Can you think of some other seeds that are good to eat?
(answer on page 23)

They are a plant's way of making sure that there will be more plants next year.

When they have grown bigger and are ripe – what happens to seeds?

a) Animals eat them

b) They fly away

c) They drop onto the ground

What happens to seeds?

When **seeds** are **ripe** they drop from their **parent plant**. Some seeds fall onto the ground below their parent plant.

If all the seeds fall into one place it will get too crowded.

So some seeds have to move away to a new place.

There will not be enough sunlight or water for the new **shoots** to grow.

Some seeds are so small they blow away in the wind.

Others grow little tufts of fluffy **down** to help them float through the air.

Some plants grow near water. Their seeds often float away to new places.

Can you think of a plant that has fluffy seeds?
(answer on page 23)

There are even plants with seed **pods** that explode, shooting the seeds onto fresh ground.

Plants get help somewhere else too. How do animals spread seeds?

a) They blow them away
b) They plant them in the garden
c) They eat them

15

How do animals spread seeds?

Lots of animals eat plants with **seeds**. The seeds come out in their **droppings**. Sometimes in a new place.

Birds collect seeds to eat. Sometimes they drop them as they fly, spreading the seeds far away.

Some seeds have little hooks. They catch on animals and travel to new places.

Even people help to spread seeds.

Children like to play with horse chestnut tree seeds. We call them conkers.

Some conkers are left on the ground in new places. They will grow into new trees.

Can you think of an animal that collects and buries seeds?
(answer on page 23)

Some of us drop apple cores with pips in.

Apple pips

The pips are seeds that can grow into apple trees.

After the summer the plants are ready for a rest. What happens to plants in winter?

a) They stop growing until the spring
b) They all die
c) They go to somewhere warm

What happens to plants in winter?

In **winter** only a few plants and trees have leaves or flowers. Most plants look as if they have died.

Their leaves fall off in **autumn** and they just have bare stems.

This is because most leaves and flowers would be hurt by winter **frost** and snow.

Can you think of a plant which keeps its leaves in winter? (answer on page 23)

But most of these plants aren't dead! They are **dormant**.

Rose bush in bloom

Dormant plants
are saving all their
energy until **spring**.
They start to grow again
when it gets warmer.

**Dormant
rose bush
in winter**

Many plants
do die, but their
seeds are safe
in the ground.

Sunflower

The seeds will
grow into a new
plant next year.

The **bulb** plants stay
safely underground
until it is spring again.

How long do plants live?

a) For hundreds of years
b) For one year
c) For more than one year

How long do plants live?

Poppies

Some plants, like poppies, live for only one year. When they die a new plant grows from a **seed** and takes their place.

Other plants and trees keep going for many years.

Rose bushes

They are **dormant** in **winter**, but each **spring** they grow back!

All plants need three things to grow. Can you think what they are?

(answer on page 23)

Some trees, like this enormous Redwood, live for hundreds of years. There is a way to tell how old a tree is.

When a tree is cut down, you can see rings in its **trunk**.

A tree grows a new ring every year. If you count the rings you can find out its age.

There is always something interesting happening in the plant world!

Glossary

Attract When a plant does something to make an insect notice it. This makes the insect want to go to the plant.

Autumn The year is divided into four parts. Autumn is the third part. Trees drop their leaves in autumn. Some plants grow their seeds in the autumn.

Bulbs Special leaves that grow very close together. Some plants grow from bulbs; they use them to store food.

Dormant Resting or not active during the winter.

Down Light and feathery parts of a seed.

Droppings Animal waste – poo!

Energy Plants, humans and animals all need energy to keep them alive. Energy makes them grow and be able to do things.

Frost A coating of ice crystals that covers everything outside when the temperature drops below freezing. Each crystal is too small to see on its own, but joined together they make everything look white.

Grind Crush into very small pieces.

In bloom When a plant is in bloom it means that it has flowers.

Insects A kind of animal that has six legs and a body in three parts. There are thousands of different kinds of insects in the world.

Nectar A sweet liquid found inside flowers that insects like to drink.

Parent plant A fully grown plant that can make seeds.

Pods Special cases or jackets that protect the seeds.

Pollen A special dust, produced by a plant. Pollen is needed to make seeds.

Ripe Ready to grow.

Seeds A small part of a plant. After the plant's flowers have died, the seeds grow. They leave the parent plant, find a new piece of ground and grow into another plant.

Shoots New growth on a plant. The first part of a plant that appears above the ground.

Spring The year is divided into four parts. Spring is the first part. Plants start to grow in the spring.

Stored When something is kept safe so that it can be used in the future.

Summer The year is divided into four parts. Summer is the second part. Plants grow flowers and seeds in the summer.

Trunk The upright part of a tree between the ground and the branches.

Winter The year is divided into four parts. Winter is the last part of the year. Some plants die in winter and some are dormant.

Could you answer all the questions? Here are the answers:

Page 6: Bulbs are made from special leaves that grow very close together.

Page 8: Lots of trees have flowers, like apple trees, horse chestnut trees and oak trees. Some tree flowers are very small.

Page 11: Bees, butterflies, wasps and moths are all good at collecting and carrying pollen.

Page 13: Lots of seeds, like sunflower seeds, are good to eat. Peas, beans and nuts are seeds too!

Page 15: Dandelions have fluffy seeds. If you blow on them you help to spread the seeds.

Page 17: Squirrels bury nuts and seeds in the ground for times when there is not enough food, like winter.

Page 18: Pine trees and holly bushes keep their leaves in winter.

Page 20: Plants need sunlight, water and carbon dioxide from the air to grow happily.

Index

t=top, b=bottom, c=centre, l=left, r=right,
OFC=outside front cover, OBC=outside back cover

Alamy: 5br, 6tl, 6c, 6br, 7tl, 7cr, 7bl, 8b, 9cr, 10, 11tr,
12tr, 12bl, 13tl, 13cl, 14tl, 15tr, 16cr, 16bl, 17cr, 17c, 19tr.
Corbis: OFC, 4tc, 4bl, 5tl, 5cb, 8tl, 11c, 12tl, 12br, 13tr,
15c, 17t, 17bl, 18tl, 18c, 20tl, 20c, 20bl, 21br.